The L.N.E.R. Scene

THE
L.N.E.R.
SCENE

An Album of photographs by
Maurice W. Earley

Oxford Publishing Co   Oxford

Oxford Publishing Co. 1973

First Published 1973
SBN 0 902888 34 X

Halftones
By Oxford Lithoplates Ltd.

Printed in the City of Oxford

Published by
Oxford Publishing Co.
5 Lewis Close
Risinghurst
Oxford.

Perhaps it was the first journey over the G.N.R. in the year 1907 that sowed the seed originally for my interest in the "L.N.E.R. Scene" in later years. That trip was from King's Cross to Louth (on the East Lincolnshire line) when the family accompanied my brother there to take up his first job. A year or two later we went up again but this time we took one of those famous fast excursions to Skegness (return fare, 3s.0d.) from King's Cross. The train I well recall was headed by a Large Atlantic (L.N.E.R. class C.1) and the coaches were vestibuled corridor stock, some of which I believe were open stock with tables — wonderful value for money! Passing Peterborough (North) station there appeared an M. & G.N. Jt. Rly. 4-4-2T standing in all its glory of "Golden ochre" livery, spotlessly clean, a sight which I can still memorise even to this day!

It was not until 1921 that the G.N.R. scene was again visited, this time at King's Cross station with a friend, making our observations at the evening rush hour. It was an unforgettable sight with train after train leaving the terminus usually headed by either an N.1 or N.2, 0-6-2T with non-corridor stock, some of which were even four- or six-wheeled, filled to capacity and in some cases with standing room only. In 1922 my first camera was used for recording some of the subjects.

Then in the year 1924, in company with the well-known railway photographer, F. E. Mackay, I started my journeys to Greenwood Box, Hadley Wood with the camera, taking the train from King's Cross to New Barnet and walking along a footpath for about three quarters of a mile to the spot. It was a perfect location with the four roads merging into two for the two track section through the tunnels; in addition the backcloth of the wood made a beautiful setting, and of course the down trains were still climbing the 1 in 200 gradient to Potter's Bar summit. No wonder this photographic spot was so popular and continued to be so until quite recent years. The journey to New Barnet sometimes had to be done by taking one of the North London Railway trains to or from Broad Street and Potter's Bar, changing at Finsbury Park for King's Cross. These were remarkable trains, headed by 4-4-0T outside cylindered engines, the coaches being 4-wheeled with half-backs to the compartments (in the third class) and bars across the door drop lights. Being constructed of teak they would have lasted for ever. In spite of all the tunnels encountered on the trips to Potter's Bar the trains were at that time (1926/28) kept remarkably clean. It was a great pity that I was far too young (in earlier days) to acquire a camera when we visited Louth as the railway subjects were most interesting. I can recall seeing the Ivatt 4-2-2's (very neat looking machines) and one or two of the G.N.R. steam rail cars, but curiously enough I cannot remember ever seeing a Stirling 8 ft. Single, although some finished their days on this line, nor can I recall a 2-4-0 of any class on our visit to Mablethorpe, but they must have been around.

From about 1936 onwards until the War my wife and I made tours by car over the East Coast route to cover L.N.E.R. subjects as far afield as Aberdeen, usually stopping at Grantham on the way home. After the War it was a case of keeping nearer home owing to petrol rationing, but we managed to cover such spots as Welwyn, Peterborough, Cromer, King's Lynn and on occasions managed to visit Grantham again. With the G.C. & G.W. Jt. Line so easily reached from Reading via High Wycombe it was possible to secure some Great Central subjects, although traffic was rather thin on that route.

That journey to Louth in 1907 gave me a feeling of great admiration and affection for the G.N. Large Atlantic (LNER class C.1) engines, and before superheating they were even more impressive as their chimneys were further back. I once possessed one of the well-known posters depicting these engines, the smokebox looming out of the picture as large as life; in subsequent editions of this poster the smokebox seemed to get bigger and bigger! Of course before the Gresley Pacifics came along the Atlantics took the lion's share of the expresses, and the roar of their exhaust coming up Potter's Bar bank was thrilling indeed, furthermore they were very photogenic; in later years they even appeared on the G.W.R. on through trains via Oxford. The L.N.E.R. was rather like the Southern in that it kept intact so many pre-Grouping classes of engines from the Constituent companies, even right up to Nationalisation days.

This was especially true of the ex G.E.R. line, so after the last War I made annual holidays in that area, covering King's Lynn, Cromer and such like. Melton Constable, however, was a most depressing scene at that time, but still full of railway interest, and probably the station itself had much of historical interest to show. Peterborough was extremely interesting with a wide variety of locomotives. Some of the trespass notices on the crossings over the line where the ex M.R. ran parallel, north of Peterborough still even bore the dates of 1898 and 1899 of King's Cross and St. Pancras, and were also freshly painted when I photographed them!

Perhaps the greatest impact that the L.N.E.R. had was the sight and sound of those splendid class N.2 Gresley 0-6-2T's on our journeys from King's Cross to New Barnet, Potter's Bar and such spots. We left London usually by one of the suburban platforms and oftentimes ran into Gas Works tunnel in company with a main-line train which had started from the other platforms. It was a case of shutting all windows, not only here but at the other tunnels northwards. In spite of all this the throaty bark of those 0-6-2T's is still very vividly recalled, and incidentally they certainly could run — lovely machines! It was very lucky that one could reach such places as New Barnet within two hours from Reading, by train, and the service was very good, especially if one caught an Inner Circle train between Paddington and King's Cross without much waiting. In the earlier days I can still remember the 0-6-2T's working through the Metropolitan line at King's Cross Underground station, with their trains from the suburbs, and of course their struggles on that fearsome gradient up to King's Cross from "under" with train loads of commuters, and that shriek of the G.N.R. whistle as the trains left the tunnels at King's Cross. The good old G.N.R. and later L.N.E.R. had a character all of its own, and the coal they used was very "tasty"! The G.N.R. even invaded the South Coast for in 1911 or 1912 my father bought me one of the cardboard publicity models of a G.N. Atlantic and its coach which were to be purchased at

A variety of chimneys at King's Cross "Top" Shed in 1954. Classes A.1 and A.4 are represented

the Enquiry Office near the front at Brighton. Those were certainly the days!!

One of our favourite "Ports of Call" was at that time (1950's) a small Hotel/Inn close by Welwyn North station and the famous viaduct. Trains passing through the night shook the bedroom, and it was only a matter of walking through a hedge to the station. This was a lovely spot, and in the 1950's we frequently walked over the south tunnel to the open space between the two tunnels, an admirable location for photography, at that period a wide open countryside and woodlands.

Even in my much younger days before 1914 there was much evidence of the G.N.R. in what was called "The Model Railway" room (actually the attic) in my parents' house. For example there was the famous poster of the G.N.R., "*Skegness is So Bracing*" featuring the dancing fisherman, one of the original versions of this famous poster. This together with a scale plan of Louth station (executed by my brother) and a G.N.R. 1914 Calendar were all on the walls of the room with the model railway in the foreground.

So you see the G.N.R. and its successor the L.N.E.R. are very much in my veins.

A.4. class 4-6-2 No.60033 *Seagull* on an up semi-fast from Cambridge passing Oakleigh Park station in 1957.

1.

A.4. class 4-6-2 No.2512 *Silver Fox* on down Silver Jubilee streamlined express passing Greenwood Box, Hadley Wood, on 26.8.36. Engine and stock in silver grey livery but the engine is without its number on the front, which was added later.

2.

"Peppercorn" class A.1 4-6-2 No.60139 *Sea Eagle* on up Yorkshire Pullman leaving Peascliffe tunnel, near Grantham, Summer 1955.

3.

A.4. class 4-6-2 No.4492 *Dominion of New Zealand* on up Flying Scotsman leaving Peascliffe tunnel, near Grantham in 1937. Engine and tender in blue livery with stainless steel numbers and lettering, also coat of arms of Dominion on cab sides. Colour light signal at entrance to tunnel ready to replace ex G.N.R. somersault type semaphore signal in foreground.

4.

2-8-2 class P.2. No.2006 *Wolf of Badenoch* on the up 3.45pm from Aberdeen near Cove Bay 23.7.38. Note the North Sea in the background, and the N.B.R. van next to the engine.

5.

G.W.R. 4-6-0 No.4079 *Pendennis Castle* backing out of King's Cross station, in company with a D.2. 4-4-0 No.4337 on April 30th 1925, during the locomotive exchanges between the two companies that year.

6.

This photograph shows engine No.1, a 0-6-0 (L.N.E.R. 'CLASS J.1) at work on a commuters train at Greenwood Box, Hadley Wood in 1924. With photograph No.43, we have shown two No.1's, the other being the Stirling 8' Single on the Special train in 1938.

7.

A large "Atlantic", class C.1, rebuilt with 4-cylinders at work on a down express passing Greenwood Box, Hadley Wood in 1925. No.3279 was rebuilt from original 2-cylinder form in 1915 and returned to this state once more in 1936.

8.

Another class C.1 large "Atlantic" working in typical style on the then 1.45pm ex King's Cross in 1926. A typical G.N.R. express train even in 1926.

9. The "Scarborough Flyer" leaving Stoke tunnel on a very hot day in August 1932. The engine is 4-6-2 No.4481 *St Simon*. The ex G.N. somersault pattern semaphore signal is very evident just above train.

10.

A variety of smoke-boxes at King's Cross "Top" Shed in 1954. Engines involved are B.1, V.2 and A.1 classes, all with steam up ready for duty.

11.

The Royal Border Bridge at Berwick on Tweed in 1937 with the up Coronation streamlined express crossing, headed by A.4. class 4-6-2 No.4489 *Dominion of Canada.*

12.

Another B.17 "Sandringham" class 4-6-0 No.2839 named then *Rendelsham Hall* (later called *Norwich City*) passing Romford with a down Cromer express in 1933. A typical ex G.E.R. six-wheeled brake is just behind the engine. The rest of the train appears to be G.E.R. bogie stock.

13.

The "Jubilee" Shed at Stratford in 1952. Engines include a B.1 4-6-0, a K.3 2-6-0 and a B.17 "Sandringham" 4-6-0. The tracks are of a typical engine shed standard!

14.

The carriage sidings at Stratford. A very interesting selection of rolling stock is evident, even to the extent of a couple of ex G.W. "Siphon" vans, an ex G.E.R. six-wheeled passenger brake, and many others — the more you look the more you find! Photograph taken in 1951.

15.

"A Helping Hand" N.2. class 0-6-2T No.69521 (L.N.E.R. No.4742) assisting the start of a main-line express at Peterborough (North) station in 1959. This station now has been largely rebuilt and so the typical G.N.R. overall roof is no longer intact.

16.

E.4. class 2-4-0 No.62788 (L.N.E.R. No.7805) with side-windowed cab fitted for working over exposed sections of line such as the Darlington—Penrith stretch. Photograph taken at Stratford Shed in 1951. This engine lasted until 1958.

17.

4-6-0 No.61139 of the B.1. class and V.2. 2-6-2 No.60912 being prepared for duty at King's Cross "Top" Shed in 1954.

18.　Ex North London Railway 4-4-0T No.2802 on a Broad Street to Potters Bar train passing through Hadley Wood in 1926. This is a poor photo but has been included to show quite clearly the bars across the door drop lights on the stock, mention of which is made in the Preface.

19.

2-8-0 Class 0.2. No.3496 pulling away from the slow road at Greenwood Box, Hadley Wood on a down freight in 1924. Of interest is the G.N.R. type bracket signal in the background with typical somersault semaphores. The engine is quite clean for this class of duty.

20.

Class J.19/2. 0-6-0 No.64666 (L.N.E.R. No.8266) of G.E.R. design but rebuilt with round-topped firebox by Gresley in 1936. The engine is just out of shops after overhaul. Photograph taken by Stratford Works in 1952.

21.

Class J.39. 0-6-0 No.4969 on down freight at Potters Bar station in 1949.

22.

Class J.15. 0-6-0 No.65435 (L.N.E.R. No.7516(of G.E.R. origin just fresh out of shops after overhaul at Stratford Shed in 1952. The engine was shedded at that time at Lowestoft. Withdrawn in 1955.

23. An ex G.C.R. 4-6-2T (L.N.E.R. class A.5) on a stopper from Marylebone to Princes Risborough in 1939. Photograph taken on G.C. & G.W. Joint line at Saunderton. Engine No.5129.

24.

An ex G.E.R. 2-4-2T of L.N.E.R. Class F.5. No.67210 (L.N.E.R. No.7109), standing outside Stratford Shed in 1952, withdrawn in 1955. The engine is obviously in a very rusty and unkempt condition.

25.

An ex G.N.R. 4-4-2T No.67386 (L.N.E.R. No.4536) of class C.12 on what appears to be Push and Pull working. Photograph taken at King's Lynn in 1956. Notice the new Diesel M.U. in the background.

26.

One of the old faithfuls for working the suburban services from King's Cross, an N.2. class 0-6-2T No.69490 (L.N.E.R. No.4606) built by the G.N.R. in December 1920. Condensing apparatus is fitted for working over the Metro lines in London. The train consists of two "Quad-Arts", the well-known articulated suburban sets of G.N.R. origin. Photograph taken in 1951, just outside Hadley Wood North tunnel.

27.

L.1. class 2-6-4T No.67730 at Stratford Sheds in 1954. Electric lighting was fitted to the class, the original of which came out in 1945 and was painted in G.N.R. green livery and numbered 9000.

28.

L.1. class 2-6-4T No.67776 on a train at Princes Risborough, a semi-fast for Marylebone in 1952. The late J. N. Maskelyne is standing near the platform edge adjusting his camera and G. W. Diesel Rail Car No.15 can be seen in the distance.

29.

Class N.7. 0-6-2T No.69624 (L.N.E.R. No.426). An L.N.E.R. version of the ex G.E.R. L77 Class Nos.1000-1011, but modified with lower cab and boiler mountings for working over the Metro line. Photograph taken at Stratford Shed in 1954.

30. Two versions of the G.E.R. ''Claud Hamilton'' Class 4-4-0 rebuilds photographed at King's Lynn in 1956. No.62606 (G.E.R. No.1 1795) has retained original style footplating etc. over coupled wheels as in photograph of 62603, but has a Gresley round-topped boiler with relevant fittings. Engine No.62575 just behind is the final form of rebuilding. In spite of their detailed differences both engines have been classified as D.16/3. by the L.N.E.R.

31. A memory of the much loved M. & G.N. Jt. Railway. A view taken at Melton Constable in 1957 with rebuilt ''Claud'' 4-4-0 No.62561 (G.E.R. No.1830) of Class D.16/3 by the shed wall, and in the distance will be seen some Class 4. L.M.S. 2-6-0's and also an ex G.E.R. Class J.15 0-6-0 peeping out of shed. Quite a mixture!

32. Ex G.N.R. Ivatt class N.1 0-6-2T No.1604 at King's Cross in 1922. Photograph taken in pre-Grouping days, hence the engine was in the G.N.R. green livery. A typical King's Cross scene of the day with a G.N.R. 0-6-0 saddle tank in background blowing off fiercely.

33.

A.4. class 4-6-2 No.60017 (L.N.E.R. No.2512) *Silver Fox* on the down Tees-Tyne Pullman express leaving Welwyn South tunnel in 1955. If compared with the shot of the same engine on the Silver Jubilee express in 1936, it will be seen that the skirting around the cylinders and motion has been removed and the engine is now in green livery, but still keeping the stainless steel replica of a fox on the boiler side. The engine has the equipment for A.W.S. fitted.

34.

A.4. class 4-6-2 No.4489 *Dominion of Canada* working the up "Flying Scotsman" at Claypole, near Newark in 1938. Engine and tender in blue livery as with 4492 in another picture. The coat of arms of the Dominion can be seen on the cab side. The Canadian Pacific Railway gave the bell just in front of the engine's chimney. There is also a most unusual ex G.N.R. somersault semaphore signal at rear of train, the lamp and spectacles are separately placed lower down the post, presumably for sighting purposes.

35.

A.4. class 4-6-2 No.60006 (L.N.E.R. No.4466) *Sir Ralph Wedgwood* on down West Riding express at Ganwick (just north of Hadley Wood North tunnel), in 1949. Engine is assumed to be in the blue livery which looks more like black in this shot! Notice the coaches at head of train, they are from one of the pre-War streamlined expresses. The original engine bearing the name *Sir Ralph Wedgwood* was virtually destroyed at York by enemy action in 1942, so No.4466 *Herring Gull* took the name instead. Skirting around cylinders and motion removed during the War for easier maintenance.

36.

A.4. class 4-6-2 No.4903 *Peregrine* (later re-named *Lord Faringdon*) on the up Yorkshire Pullman at Claypole, in the summer of 1938. The engine is in blue livery and equipped with double chimney.

4-6-2 (as original class A.1) No.2554 *Woolwinder* on down 4pm ex King's Cross near Potters Bar in 1929. The train consists largely of ex G.N.R. clerestory roofed corridor stock.

38. B.7. class 4-6-0 No.469, an ex Great Central engine, a mixed traffic version of the famous 4-cylinder express passenger engines of "Lord Faringdon" class. The train is interesting as the stock is of the Tourist/Excursion sets built in 1933 especially for that type of work. The coaches are classless and are of open stock with bucket type seats, two Buffet Cars are provided with each rake and some coaches are in articulated sets. Livery is green lower and cream upper panels with white roofs, quite a unique development in L.N.E.R. coach design at that time.

39.

In early L.N.E.R. days another class N.1. 0-6-2T at King's Cross station. The engine still bears original G.N. numbering (No.1599) but is in the current black livery for this class and is standing on exactly the same road as No.1604 in another photograph. Photo taken in 1924.

40.

Starting off from King's Lynn in 1956 we have a Gresley D.16/3 rebuild of the ex G.E.R. "Claud Hamilton" Class 4-4-0's, this time No.62575 (G.E.R. No.1824). In middle road on left is seen an ex G.N.R. 4-4-2T (L.N.E.R. Class C.12). Incidentally this train has reversed at King's Lynn and another rebuilt "Claud" is to be seen detached at end of train.

41.

A typical G.N.R. Commuters train of the 1920's. A 4-4-0 of Class L.N.E.R. D.2., numbered 4387 heads an outer-suburban stopper past Greenwood Box, at Hadley Wood in 1924. The rolling stock is most interesting as it shows a couple of low-roofed G.N.R. Gresley articulated twins, plus a massive collection of 6-wheeled coaches behind. Note lamp on top of Guard's look-out in first coach and the short destination boards.

42.

An ex G.E.R. "Claud Hamilton" class 4-4-0 No.8848 (L.N.E.R. Class D.16/3) as rebuilt by Gresley with round topped firebox, the footplating modified over the coupled wheels, a wider cab and standard L.N.E.R. Gresley design chimney fitted. This was the first engine of the class to be so rebuilt and came out in January 1933. Photograph taken in August of that year on a train for Southend. Please note the ancient 6-wheeled non-corridor coaching stock still in service!

43. A famous historical Special. G.N.R. 8′ Single No.1 (built in 1870) preserved after being taken out of service in 1907, and subsequently renovated after a repose in York Museum. Photograph taken on Sept. 11th 1938 when No.1 was used to work a Special comprised of ''period'' Flying Scotsman stock of seven six-wheeled coaches (organised by the R.C. & T.S.). The following train was of modern stock hauled by an A.4 Gresley ''Pacific'' — quite a comparison. Note the background of trees in this picture, the same spot as in picture 69. These trees were largely destroyed by enemy action in the last War.

44. ''Peppercorn'' class A.1. 4-6-2 No.60117 *Bois Roussel* on an up fast leaving Hadley Wood North Tunnel in 1952. The first coach appears to be of G.C.R. vintage.

45.

This time a couple of "Directors" (Class D.11) Nos.62665/62666, (L.N.E.R. Nos.5501/5502) *Mons and Zeebrugge* respectively, on the "Farnborough Flyer" Special approaching Basingstoke from the G.W. Reading branch on a dull day in Sept. 1955.

46.

One of the splendid N.E.R. "R" class (L.N.E.R. Class D.20) 4-4-0's at work on a stopping train at Alnmouth in 1939. This engine No.2029 was built in 1900, a member of a very capable class of 4-4-0's designed by Wilson Worsdell. Photograph depicts the engine at head of a complete train of ex N.E.R. stock.

47.

4-6-2 No.4474 (then un-named but later *Victor Wild*) at work on the 1.30pm ex Paddington—Plymouth express passing Sonning Signal Box near Reading, during pre-test runs in the 1925 Locomotive Exchange between the L.N.E.R. and the G.W.R.

48.

Ex N.B.R. "Scott" class 4-4-0 (L.N.E.R. Class D.30) No.9413 named *Caleb Balderstone* on an up fast from Aberdeen at Portlethen, near Cove Bay in 1938. The signal standing up behind the train savours strongly of Caledonian Railway origin.

49.

One of the famous "Director" class 4-4-0's (Class D.11) No.5510 *Princess Mary* on the up "Queen of Scots" Pullman near Grantham in August 1932. The tall spire of Grantham Church stands out prominently on the sky-line.

50.

Class C.7. 4-4-2, ex-N.E.R., No.2202 (N.E.R. class Z) a 3-cylinder simple engine, at work on the 10.30am Edinburgh—Newcastle fast. Photograph taken in 1938 at Burnmouth, just north of the Border in Berwickshire. The engine had original Westinghouse pump taken out; screw reverse fitted. The North Sea is just beyond the headland on the right and at that time bathers seemed to make the railway a short cut to the sea!

51. Double-headed out of Aberdeen. N.B.R. 4-4-0 No.9423, class L.N.E.R. D.30, *Quentin Durward* and "Shire" class D.49, 4-4-0 No.270 *Argyllshire* on an up express. According to the old N.B.R. practice the train engine works as a pilot, hence the N.B.R. 4-4-0 next to the train. Photo taken near Cove Bay in 1938.

52.

Post-War grime but still in full cry. Large "Atlantic" No.4410 on a down Hitchin semi-fast at Ganwick in 1946; it will be noticed that wind shields have been fitted to cab sides to assist enginemen, when looking out.

53.

Large "Atlantic" No.3272 on humble duty with a stopping train leaving Potters Bar in 1931. A lovely variety of ex G.N. coaching stock on this train, just examine the picture closely and see!

54.

Large "Atlantic" No.3284 leaves Stoke tunnel with the up West Riding Pullman on the hottest day of August 1932 when the temperature was reputed to be 100 F in the shade in London. With my friend Frank Carrier I had WALKED five miles from Grantham to reach this spot that day, and it was over 80 F here in Lincolnshire. Another beautifully kept engine, not surprising as this was one of the "top class" duties at that time with the Pullmans.

55.

One of the small Atlantics, class C.2. and often called "Klondykes" in their early days. Here we see 3949 heading an up stopper from Hitchin and leaving Hadley Wood South tunnel, by Greenwood Box, in August 1936.

56.

Another small Atlantic, class C.2. making heavy weather and slipping badly (see sand at coupled wheels), leaving the tunnel at Wood Green with an empty stock train in 1930. Engine No.3982, built 1900, withdrawn in Nov. 1935.

57.

The first British Atlantic locomotive ex G.N.R. No.990 (L.N.E.R. No.3990) "Henry Oakley" built 1898, withdrawn from service in October 1937 and preserved at York Museum. This photograph shows No.990 at work on a Grantham—Boston stopper, near Grantham on 31st July 1937 and must have been on some of her final duties in traffic. Quite an ex G.N.R. ensemble with the bracket somersault semaphore signal, a Gresley twin articulated set and an old G.N.R. coach at rear!

58.

Original British Atlantic No.990 of G.N.R. seen here as preserved at York Museum, 28th July 1938, in company with many other historical relics. Not much time lost in her restoration and preservation in the twelve months between the two shots of her.

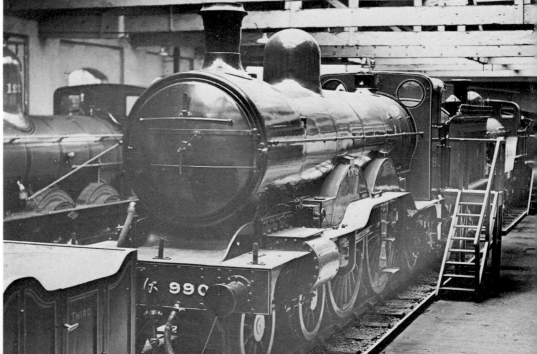

59.

"The One and Only" 4-6-2-2 No.10000 as rebuilt from the original experimental high pressure 4-cylinder Compound of 1929. It is seen here heading an up express from Harrogate, near Claypole in 1938, engine and tender in blue livery. This locomotive was rebuilt into the form here in 1937 with boiler similar to the A.4 Pacifics but with larger firebox. The distant signal of the G.N.R. somersault pattern, with lamp and spectacles lower in post, can be seen at rear of train.

60.

2-6-0 class K.3. No.61853 (L.N.E.R. No.180) at work on a "Coal Drag" leaving Potters Bar tunnel in 1951. The engine is absolutely filthy but drifting smoke has outlined quite a variety of wagon stock on this train.

61.

K.2. class 2-6-0 No.61767 (L.N.E.R. 4677, G.N.R. 1677) built by the North British Loco. Co. in 1918. A typical ex G.N.R. design, including the cab and boiler fittings although strictly a Gresley design. Photograph taken at Stratford in 1951.

62.

Another K.3 class 2-6-0 on the well-known "Scotch" Goods, or 3.30pm King's Cross—Niddrie fast goods, at Ganwick in 1946. Engine does not appear to have any visible number especially on buffer-beam, but records suggest it is L.N.E.R. 28.

63.   4-6-2 No.2547 *Doncaster* (as then class A.1.) on a down express for Newcastle passing through Hadley Wood in 1932. The engine and tender of course are in L.N.E.R. green but notice how it gleams in even a poor light of a dull day when kept in such a spotless condition.

64. The original large "Atlantic" No.3251 (now preserved) at work on an up Scarborough fast near Grantham in 1932. The spotless condition of the engine is outstanding even in those much cleaner days, possibly a Grantham engine!

65.

An ex G.E.R. "Super Claud" (L.N.E.R. Class D.16/2) No.62603 (G.E.R. 1792) at Stratford on 2nd Sept. 1951. As this engine was withdrawn during the same month it is possible that the photograph is the last one taken of her.

66.

Another V.2. class 2-6-2 No.4793 at work on an Edinburgh—Aberdeen express at Portlethen in summer 1938.

67.

Another Gresley rebuild of G.E.R. "Claud" (L.N.E.R. Class D.16/3) 4-4-0 No.62516 (G.E.R.1855) at Stratford Works in 1954. Engine is apparently shedded at King's Lynn the home of so many representatives of these engines, in all their various states of modification.

68.

A batch of B.12/3's at home at Cromer shed in 1957.

69.

The rebuilt 4-6-2 L.N.E.R. 4470 now re-numbered as 113 working the down Yorkshire Pullman (if one can read the headboard!) just having left Hadley Wood North tunnel on a hot summer's day in 1948. The heat of the day and highly superheated steam has rendered exhaust invisible against a brilliant blue sky.

70.

Large ''Atlantic'', class C.1, No.3283 on an up Leeds express at Saltersford, nr. Grantham on a very hot day in the August of 1932. One of the ''back-room boys'' of Derby Works, Frank Carrier, is at work with his camera.

71.

V.2. class 2-6-2 No.3663 (later No.60936) on a down Cleethorpes fast between the tunnels just north of Hadley Wood station, photographed in 1946.

72.

One of the big army of mixed traffic 4-6-0's introduced by Thompson in 1942, class B.1, and numbered in the 10xx series. Here we see No.61142 on a fast for Cleethorpes between the tunnels at Ganwick, north of Hadley Wood station. Photograph taken in 1951.

73.

B.12/3 ex G.E.R. 4-6-0 No.61580 (L.N.E.R. 8580) as rebuilt by Gresley with larger boiler and round-topped firebox etc. The locomotive is in the then standard black livery photographed in 1954 when fresh from shops at Stratford. A very handsome looking 4-6-0.

74.

B.2. class 4-6-0 rebuilt from a "Sandringham" class B.17. into a two-cylinder machine around 1945/46. It is named *Royal Sovereign* and numbered 61671 usually being kept at that time in fine condition for possible Royal Train duties. Photograph taken in 1955 with the engine leaving Welwyn North tunnel with an up fast from Cambridge.

75.

A Ministry of Supply, "Austerity" 2-8-0 No.78709 on an up coal train leaving Potter's Bar tunnel in 1946. This engine was built by the Vulcan Foundry in 1944 for War service, landed in Germany and then returned to England for service on the L.N.E.R. in December 1945.

76.

Class C.4. 4-4-2 from Great Central Railway heading the 12.15pm Marylebone—Manchester fast, via High Wycombe, near Saunderton on the G.W. & G.C. Joint line in August 1932. The beautiful lines of these G.C. "Atlantics" are rather spoiled by the L.N.E.R. modified chimney.

77.

"Sandringham" class 4-6-0 No.61655 (L.N.E.R. No.2855) *Middlesbrough* of the "Football" series on a down Cambridge semi-fast passing Hadley Wood station in 1952.

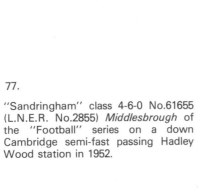

78.

A Thompson pattern class A.2/1 of 4-6-2 No.508 (original No.3697) subsequently named *Duke of Rothesay* on a down fast for Harrogate. Photograph taken in 1946 just south of the Potters Bar tunnel. The engine is equipped with wing type smoke deflectors; electric lighting is not fitted to this engine of the class.

79.

Class A.1, (later A.3.) 4-6-2 No.2565 *Merry Hampden* on the up "Queen of Scots" Pullman express at Burnmouth just north of the border in Berwickshire. The North Sea can be seen beyond headland on the right. Photograph taken in 1938.

80.

Rear view of A.3. class 4-6-2 No.2750 *Papyrus* on a down Leeds express entering Peascliffe tunnel near Grantham in the year 1937. Notice the immaculate condition of both engine and tender, the latter being of the corridor pattern.

81. The original Gresley Pacific *Great Northern* rebuilt out of recognition by Thompson (L.N.E.R. 4470) standing at King's Cross station at the head of the "Aberdonian" in April 1946. It was a wet dirty evening, typical of this station in such weather in the steam days, making photography difficult at 7.30pm. The engine is equipped with electric lighting, and the white discs for daylight use. The livery is blue.

82. B.17 "Sandringham" class 4-6-0 No.2836 *Harlaxton Manor* on a down Yarmouth express passing
Romford in August 1933. Train consists of largely ex G.E.R. stock.

83.

Class A.3. 4-6-2 No.60097 (L.N.E.R. No.2751) *Humorist* on the down 1pm "Scotsman" from King's Cross leaving Hadley Wood North tunnel, in 1949. The engine has double chimney and smoke deflectors.

84.

Class A.3. 4-6-2 No.2744 *Grand Parade* on the down 3pm ex-King's Cross to Cromer etc. express near Potters Bar in 1929. There is a nice selection of pure ex G.N.R. rolling stock on this train, plus the somersault semaphore pattern bracket signal in the rear of the train.

85.

A.3. class 4-6-2 No.2795 *Call Boy* on the up non-stop "Flying Scotsman" photographed near Grantham in 1932 with a very neat set of coaches especially rostered for this service. The locomotive and tender are in L.N.E.R. green, of course, and with corridor tender.

86.

A.3. class 4-6-2 No.E.112 (L.N.E.R. No.4481) *St. Simon* on the up Yorkshire Pullman express leaving Potter's Bar tunnel in 1948. The locomotive and tender are nice and clean in green livery with "British Railways" on the tender, the "E" in front of the number indicating an ex L.N.E.R. engine before finally being re-numbered in the 60xxx series. A fine rake of Pullmans and a clean engine made an attractive ensemble.

88.	B.12 (G.E.R. 1500 class) 4-6-0 No.8547 on the down second part of what was originally called "Norfolk Coast Express", taken in August 1933 at Romford. The second coach from the engine is a non-corridor 6-wheeled coach of G.E.R. origin. Compare this shot of a B.12 in original condition with picture No.73 which is of the rebuilt version (engine No.61580).

87.

Peppercorn A.1 "Pacific" No.60125 *Scottish Union* working the well-known Scotch Goods, 3.30pm ex King's Cross—Niddrie fast freight. Photograph taken at Oakleigh Park in 1957. The engine is very clean, possibly running-in after an overhaul.

89.

P.1. class 2-8-2 No.2394 on an up mineral train at Greenwood Box, Hadley Wood in 1926. These massive engines proved far too competent for the work for which they were designed, the moving of 100 wagon coal trains between New England and Ferme Park. Such lengthy trains were too much for many of the loops and sidings on this stretch, so their power was wasted. It will be noted that the engine is fitted with a booster on the rear truck. Photograph taken in very poor light in early April but the subject was too good to miss!

90.

A.4. class 4-6-2 No.60033 (L.N.E.R. No.4902) *Seagull* on the post-War Edinburgh—London non-stop "Elizabethan" express, photographed between the tunnels at Welwyn in 1955. The engine is in green livery and coaches in the current "plum and spilt milk" colours of B.R. The engine is fitted with A.W.S. type equipment. Plenty of coal is left on the tender after that long run.

91.   The last of the "Atlantics" of the G.N.R. Here we have No.62822 (L.N.E.R. No.3294) at Doncaster
on Nov. 26th, 1950 after working her last duty, the "Ivatt Atlantic Special". Just after this
photograph was taken the engine passed over to the "Plant" yards for a short exhibition which
included the original large "Atlantic" No.251, after which it went to the scrap yard. Although her
final trip, 62822 did the journey in typical "Atlantic" style, in spite of fog in the London area.

The author would like to express his sincere thanks to the London North Eastern Railway Company and its successors, the Eastern Region of British Railways, for their kind and ready assistance which has enabled him to take so many pictures over the past years, not forgetting the many valued friends he has made amongst the railwaymen, and the many enjoyable hours spent with them on "location".